# Stepping Into the Light

## Healing Stress and Anxiety Through Self Connection

## Table of Contents

| | |
|---|---|
| Foreword | 2 |
| Chapter 1 - Understanding Stress and Anxiety | 4 |
| Chapter 2 Building Resilience | 16 |
| Chapter 3 Taming Your Inner Critic | 25 |
| Chapter 4 Boosting Self-Esteem | 33 |
| Chapter 5 Mastering Time Management | 41 |
| Chapter 6 Decluttering Your Life | 50 |
| Chapter 7 Sleeping Deeply | 60 |
| Chapter 8 Eating for Energy and Health | 67 |
| Chapter 9 Moving Your Body | 74 |
| Chapter 10 Cultivating Connections | 81 |
| Chapter 11 Practising Mindfulness | 88 |
| Chapter 12 Seeking Help When Needed | 96 |
| Appendix one UK Resources | 100 |
| Appendix Two Global Resources | 102 |
| Appendix Three Key Coping Techniques | 104 |
| References | 107 |

-

## Foreword:

Life moves fast. Our inboxes overflow, smartphones ding incessantly, and our calendars fill quickly with obligations both personal and professional. The rapid pace of modern life often feels more like a turbulent white-water rapid than a peaceful stream. This book is a lifeline to help you navigate daily turbulence and find calm in the chaos.

Within these pages, you'll learn pragmatic techniques to manage stress, quiet inner critics, boost self-esteem, declutter, improve sleep habits, nourish your body, cultivate connections, tap into mindfulness, and so much more. Consider this book your oasis and respite from the rush and strain of everyday demands.

Calm the Chaos is rooted in mindfulness, which simply means paying purposeful attention to the present moment. Research shows mindfulness practices reduce anxiety, improve focus, and promote overall wellbeing. By tuning into the here-and now, you can respond more thoughtfully instead of reactively. Small daily mindful moments can ripple into greater peace of mind.

This book provides bite-sized strategies you can fit into a busy schedule. Keep it by your bedside for evening inspiration. Tuck it in your bag for on-the-go centring. Share favourite chapters with friends and family. Use it as a touchstone for self-care and sanity. Consider me your guide, but remember, it is you who holds the power to redirect the Frenzy of the white-water into the flow of the stream.

Together we'll find stillness within motion, cling less tightly trying to control the uncontrollable, and release attachment to perfect outcomes. You'll uncover what matters most and move toward it one mindful step after another. Even on the most chaotic days, you can tap into an inner wellspring of calm. My hope is that this book will show you how.

So, whenever you feel overwhelmed, take a deep breath, open these pages, and let's begin calming the chaos, one day at a time.

# Chapter 1: Understanding Stress and Anxiety

In this chapter we will look at the following elements relating stress and anxiety.

**The physiology of stress**

Stress and anxiety are intricately intertwined experiences that impact our daily lives. In this chapter, we will explore the physiological mechanisms behind these emotions, common triggers that exacerbate symptoms, and evidence-based techniques to find relief.

**What is Stress?**

Stress is defined as the body's response to perceived threats or demands. When we encounter stressors, our sympathetic nervous system activates, triggering the fight-or-flight response. The hypothalamus signals the adrenal glands to release stress hormones like cortisol and adrenaline. These hormones generate a cascade of physiological changes, including increased heart rate, blood pressure, and respiration.

Glucose is released to supply the body with energy. Perspiration increases to cool the skin. The pupils dilate to improve vision. Digestion shuts down as blood diverts to the muscles. This prepares us to confront threats by fighting or fleeing.

Stress evolved as an adaptive response to danger. Our ancestors relied on these reactions to cope with predators and other environmental threats. However, in the modern world, stress often stems from psychological stressors like work pressure, financial strain, or relationship conflicts. Prolonged or excessive stress can lead to burnout, anxiety disorders, depression, and worsening physical health. Understanding the neuroscience behind stress empowers us to modulate our reactions.

## What Triggers Stress?

Stress arises in response to stressors. These can be events, situations, environments, or emotions that the brain interprets as challenging, harmful, or threatening. Common examples include:

- Workplace stressors: heavy workload, tight deadlines, job insecurity, issues with coworkers

- Financial stressors: debt, low income, unforeseen expenses

- Health stressors: chronic illness, injuries, poor diet, lack of exercise

- Relationship stressors: conflict, social isolation, domestic abuse, parenting challenges, loss of loved ones

- Environmental stressors: noise pollution, extreme weather, natural disasters

-

- Internal stressors: pessimism, perfectionism, lack of work-life balance, rumination

While external stressors are abundant, our individual appraisals and coping resources determine whether a situation becomes stressful. Two people can interpret the same event very differently. Resilience factors like optimism, social support, and healthy habits protect against stress. Those lacking in these areas are more vulnerable. High levels of uncertainty also magnify stress. The COVID-19 pandemic has been an unsettling example, disrupting routines and sparking health and financial fears for many.

Understanding your personal stressors is the first step in prevention. Keep a journal tracking your moods, situations, and stress levels. Over time, patterns will emerge revealing your common triggers. Develop strategies to modify or avoid these stressors where possible. Bolstering resilience through rest, relationships, and self-care can further arm you against unnecessary stress.

**The Physiology of Anxiety**

Anxiety is closely tied to stress, as sustained or repetitive stress can manifest as chronic anxiety. Anxiety disorders now impact 1 in 5 people, making this mental health condition highly prevalent worldwide.

During acutely stressful events, anxiety generates similar physiological arousal to the fight-or-flight response. Heart rate and blood pressure rise. Breathing quickens. Muscles tense. This prepares us to confront threats. However, in anxiety disorders, these reactions recur frequently and disproportionately, often in the absence of real danger.

Brain imaging studies reveal several regions involved in generating anxiety. The amygdala activates the sympathetic nervous system, triggering anxiety's physical symptoms. When the prefrontal cortex perceives risk, it signals the amygdala to initiate the stress response. However, in anxiety disorders, a hypersensitive amygdala overreacts to benign stimuli, sounding the alarm even without genuine threats.

The hippocampus normally encodes memories and contextualises risk, but its integration is impaired in anxiety. As a result, those with anxiety disorders struggle to recall safety signals and override amygdala alarms. Reduced serotonin and GABA levels also disinhibit anxiety activation pathways.

Understanding neuroscience highlights that anxiety is an overprotective mechanism. Reframing anxiety as an exaggerated safety response can help sufferers relate to their symptoms with greater compassion. It also empowers us to target key neural pathways with therapies and lifestyle changes to recalibrate an irregular stress reaction.

-

**Impacts of Unmanaged Stress and Anxiety.**

Unmanaged stress and anxiety exact both a psychological and physiological toll. Research reveals far-reaching impacts on our mental health, brain, and body when left unchecked.

Mental health:

Over time, unrelenting stress and anxiety increase risks for:

- Clinical depression or other mood disorders

- Addiction, substance abuse

- Burnout

- Suicidal ideation


**Effects on the Brain:**

- Memory and concentration impairment

- Reduced capacity for learning and decision-making

- Structural changes like dendritic atrophy and reduced grey matter

- Diminished neuroplasticity and neurogenesis


**Effects on Physical health:**

- Impaired immune function and frequent sickness

- Headaches, back pain, muscle tension

- High blood pressure, heart disease

- Digestive issues like irritable bowel syndrome

- Diabetes and obesity

- Accelerated biological ageing

The cascading consequences underscore the vital need to manage anxiety and stress effectively. Seeking early treatment and outlets for stress protects both physical and mental health. This prevents benign symptoms from developing into clinical disorders. Lifestyle changes further help reverse the toll of stress on the brain and body.

**Recognizing Your Personal Stress Signals**

Since individuals experience stress differently, identifying your personal symptoms is key for prompt intervention. Monitoring physical sensations, thought patterns, and behaviours can reveal unique early warning signs that stress or anxiety is building.

**Common physical signals include:**

- Headaches, muscle tension

- Fatigue, insomnia, poor concentration

- Upset stomach, nausea, constipation or diarrhoea

- Increased heart rate, sweating

- Frequent sickness and infections

-

**Mental symptoms may involve:**

- Feeling irritable, impatient, on-edge

- Increased negative thinking

- Worrying excessively

- Difficulty concentrating  - Intrusive thoughts, rumination

    Behavioural signals involve:

- Avoiding interactions or activities

- Snapping at others when irritated

- Increased fidgeting or restlessness

- Difficulty starting or completing tasks

- Using alcohol, drugs, or food for comfort

Tuning into personal warning signs equips individuals to take swift action in mitigating stress. Strategies like taking a walk, calling a friend, practising deep breathing, or scheduling a therapy session can defuse rising anxiety when caught early. Identifying red flags also helps pinpoint specific stressors to modify. Those aware of their signals stay vigilant for unhealthy escalation.

**Healthy Ways to Cope with Stress**

When stress surfaces, how we respond makes all the difference. Engaging in unhealthy coping strategies like smoking, overeating, lashing out at others, or avoidance often backfire, amplifying stress over time. Alternatively, the following evidence-based techniques reliably curb anxiety:

Exercise - Aerobic exercise releases endorphins, improves sleep, and reduces muscle tension. Even brief walks benefit mood.

Meditation and breath-work - Centring practices clear the mind, slow racing thoughts, and cultivate calm. Deep breathing triggers relaxation.

CBT and mindfulness - Reframing cognitive distortions lessens perceived threats. Mindfulness revives presence.

Progressive muscle relaxation- Cycling muscle tension and release alleviate full-body strain.

Laughing and smiling - Mirthful laughter lowers stress hormones like cortisol. Smiling activates happiness pathways.

Music, art, nature - Soothing music, creative expression, and natural settings promote serenity. Nature walks refresh.

Supportive connections - Relating with empathetic listeners bolsters resilience. Social bonds meet our need to belong.

-

Healthy habits - good sleep, nutrition and limiting alcohol/caffeine fortifies us to withstand stressors.

By experimenting to find which coping mechanisms resonate best, individuals can assemble a toolkit of trusted techniques.
With consistent practice stress becomes more manageable.

Even five to ten minutes of deep breathing or meditation during stressful days makes a difference long-term.


**Seeking Therapy for Anxiety Disorders**

Those experiencing chronic, debilitating anxiety linked with panic attacks, compulsive behaviours or overwhelming dread may benefit from therapy and psychiatric intervention. Evidence-based modalities include:

Cognitive behavioural therapy (CBT) - CBT focuses on unlearning anxious thought patterns and behaviours. Exposure
therapy progressively reduces fear triggers in a safe environment.


Acceptance commitment therapy (ACT) - ACT teaches anxious minds to accept difficult thoughts and feelings rather than over-identifying with them.

Mindfulness-based therapies - These therapies strengthen present moment awareness and self-acceptance to short-circuit anxiety. Mindfulness-Based Stress Reduction (MBSR) is one renowned approach.

Medication - SSRIs, SNRIs, benzodiazepines may be prescribed for severe anxiety, especially when paired with therapy.

Psychiatric care is strongly recommended for individuals experiencing anxiety that severely constricts quality of life.

Combining medications and therapeutic modalities often provides lasting relief from excessive anxiety.

**Relapse Prevention Through Lifestyle Changes**

Implementing key lifestyle changes enhances the benefits of therapy over the long-term. Poor health habits exacerbate anxiety, while wellness practices help stabilise mood. Consider the following:

Regular exercise - At least 30 minutes per day keeps anxiety at bay by reducing muscle tension, boosting endorphins and improving sleep.

Healthy diet - Limiting caffeine, alcohol, refined sugar and processed foods prevents energy crashes. Anti-inflammatory foods like fatty fish, berries and leafy greens nourish mental health.

-

Good sleep hygiene - Adults require 7-9 hours of quality sleep for emotional regulation. Restore natural circadian rhythms by turning off screens before bed.

Stress management - Routinely build in relaxing activities like light yoga, enjoyable hobbies and buffered time between tasks. Say no to overwhelming demands.

Gratitude and savouring - Notice positive moments and direct appreciation toward your life and loved ones to cultivate joy and meaning.

Nature exposure - Spend time outdoors. Studies confirm that being in nature bolsters mood for hours.

Mindfulness meditation - Even a few minutes daily strengthens emotional resilience by anchoring us in the present.

Social connection - Nurture fulfilling relationships and limit time with toxic people. Loneliness exacerbates anxiety.

By incorporating lifestyle changes consistent with your needs and preferences, you can chart a holistic course for mastering anxiety. Consistency is key - anxiety improves gradually through daily upkeep of wellbeing habits over months. Be patient and celebrate small wins.

## In Summary

Our deep dive into the intricacies of stress and anxiety reveals the nuanced nature of these ubiquitous emotions. While often adaptive in small doses, uncontrolled stress can morph into debilitating anxiety and long-term health consequences. The good news is that understanding the underlying drivers of anxiety empowers us to moderate its impact. Through lifestyle tweaks, therapeutic techniques, and a compassionate relationship with your symptoms, a life of greater ease, joy and purpose awaits. Now equipped with a comprehensive understanding of stress, forge ahead with optimism and begin practising research-backed coping strategies tailored to your needs.

## Chapter 2: Building Resilience

Resilience is the capacity to withstand adversity and bounce back from difficult life events. In our complex world, challenges await around every corner. Thus, cultivating resilience emerges as a vital skill for maintaining wellbeing and finding meaning amidst hardship.

This chapter unpacks the foundations of resilience, how to grow it, and how to tap into its power to navigate life's inevitable ups and downs. Drawing on psychology research and lived experiences, we will explore strategies for constructing a resilient mind-set and facing trials with courage. By building emotional, social and physical resilience reserves, you can approach your future with confidence.

### What is Resilience?

Resilience is defined as the ability to adapt well in the face of trauma, tragedy, health problems, financial stress, relationship issues, and other adversities. Resilient individuals exhibit an uncanny ability to bounce back and even grow stronger after stressful events. However, resilience is not an innate, fixed trait. It involves behaviours, thoughts and actions that can be intentionally fostered.

**Markers of resilience include:**

Managing stress and regulating emotions under pressure

- Staying composed, focused and flexible when faced with change

- Accepting circumstances beyond your control

- Persevering through challenges and setbacks

- Maintaining overall good health despite hardship

- Retaining hope and optimism even amid loss or failure

- Emerging from adversity with greater wisdom and meaning

These qualities demonstrate that resilience is a complex web of mental manoeuvres, social supports and self-care rituals that equip us to weather storms. With consistent practice, resilient responses can become habits that provide an emotional anchor.

**Why is Resilience Important?**

Resilience is crucial for long-term wellbeing as adversity is inevitable in life. Setbacks such as job losses, illnesses, deaths of loved ones and disasters impact everyone at some point. However, research reveals resilient individuals consistently enjoy greater physical health, mental health and life satisfaction.

-

**By strengthening resilience, you can:**

- Moderate your stress response and prevent burnout

- Lessen the emotional impact of hardships

- Recover faster after traumatic events or illness

- Adapt well to changing life circumstances

- Persist through repeated failures to achieve goals

- Maintain overall wellness habits despite challenges

- Derive meaning from painful losses and experiences

In contrast, those lacking resilience get derailed by obstacles. They struggle to process change, loss and disappointment. Minor stressors trigger exaggerated reactions. Each new challenge chips away at their reserves. Bolstering resilience provides a buffer so life's turbulence cannot sink you.


**Cultivating Resilient Mind-sets**

Our mind-sets and thought patterns largely shape how we appraise challenges and setbacks. Certain outlooks foster resilience, while others undermine our ability to cope. By adjusting key thought habits, you can build up mental resilience.

-        **Practice optimism** – Interpret situations positively and maintain hope for the future, even during trials. This sustains motivation.

-      **Accept what cannot change** – Flow with circumstances beyond your control to reduce suffering. Changing the unchangeable is exhausting.

-      **Focus on personal growth** – Look for lessons and meaning in difficulties. How can this make you wiser?

-      **Maintain perspective** – Keep setbacks in perspective. How significant will this be in five years? Avoid exaggerated thinking.

-      **Celebrate small wins** – Recognize accomplishments, no matter how minor. Small progress sustains momentum.


-      **Limit negative self-talk** – Avoid excessive rumination and blaming yourself for challenges. Be kind to yourself.

-      **Envision success** – Visualise yourself overcoming obstacles. Imagine the future you want. These build resolves.

Adjusting mind-sets requires mindfulness, as automatic thoughts easily revert to familiar patterns. With practice, resilience-building mindsets rise to the forefront when you need them.

-

### Social Resilience: The Power of Relationships

Connections with others are foundational for coping with adversity. Loneliness and isolation leave us vulnerable when trials strike. By proactively nurturing relationships and asking for support we strengthen resilience.

### Ways to build social resilience include:

**- Surround yourself with positive people**

– Limit time with those who undermine confidence. Shared positivity uplifts.

**- Give and receive support**

– Serve others and allow loved ones to help carry your burdens too. We all need assistance sometimes.

**- Join community groups**

– Find joy and meaning through volunteer work, classes, activities, faith communities or mutual interest groups.

**- Open up about struggles**

– Confiding in trusted friends and asking for help when needed fosters understanding. Suppressing emotions Heightens isolation.

**- Practice forgiveness**

– Let go of grudges and bitterness toward others. Forgiveness lifts your spirit and frees you from negativity.

**Be a source of hope**

– Share your experiences overcoming adversity to give hope to others facing trials. Our lives can be lessons.

Social resilience replenishes us with positive energy to overcome challenges. Shared laughter, hugs, kind words and quality time forge bonds that shield us from despair. Seek people who uplift and avoid draining relationships. Mutual support makes hardship bearable.

**Physical Resilience: Fortify Your Body and Spirit**

Attending basic self-care fortifies reserves of physical resilience when trials arise. Emotional struggles impact the body. By listening to your body's needs and establishing healthy routines, you prime your system to handle taxing situations.

**Ways to build physical resilience include:**

-       **Reduce unhealthy habits** – Limit alcohol use, processed/sugary foods, drugs, and poor sleep. These deplete energy and mood.

-       **Exercise daily** – Aim for 30 minutes a day. It releases endorphins, manages weight, and improves sleep quality.

-

- **Practice meditation** – Quiet the mind, reduce anxiety/depression, lower blood pressure, boost mood. Try yoga and deep breathing too.

- **Spend time in nature** – Fresh air, greenery and sunlight lift spirits. Feel your connection to the living world.

- **Express yourself creatively** – Make art, play music, write in a journal. Creative release provides an emotional outlet.

- **Take vacations** – Plan regular getaways to unwind and explore life. New sights inject wonder and joy.

- **Receive bodywork** – Massage, acupuncture and other modalities reduce muscle tension caused by chronic stress.

When your basic self-care needs are met, you have greater capacity to handle challenges. Do not neglect your health. Listen to your body and give it what it asks for - rest, nourishment, movement and soul-filling activities.

### Finding Growth and Meaning in Adversity

With resilience, we transcend merely surviving adversity, also using challenges as catalysts for profound growth. Times of difficulty often open windows to previously undiscovered wisdom, strength and purpose within ourselves.

- **Let go of control** – Accept that life is uncertain. Relinquish the need to control everything. Go with the flow. What happens has value even if it was unintended.

- **Help others** – Assisting those facing similar trials gives your experience meaning. Turn wounds into wisdom that heals others.

- **Reframe obstacles** – Look at trials as teachers rather than punishers. Each one builds character and reveals truths about life. Difficulties compel growth.

- **Practise gratitude** – Be thankful for what remains rather than focusing on loss. Gratitude is powerful medicine, dissolving resentment.

- **Explore new paths** – When one door closes, find open windows. Let go of past attachments and experiment with novel directions when old ones close off.

- **Write your story** – Draft a redemption narrative of your journey. How have setbacks shaped you? What insights have they revealed? Where did you find courage?

- **Commit to change** – Let difficulties motivate positive change. Dedicate yourself to lifelong learning and creating good from harm.

With openness and courage, we can ascribe meaning to suffering and write the next victorious chapter in our ever unfolding story. There is light ahead.

## In Summary

Hardships inevitably arise, but the resilient remain unshaken, flexibly adapting to whatever may come. Through mindset adjustments, strong social networks and self-care, resilience buffers stress. It is not an innate trait, but a lifelong practice.

Anyone willing can foster resilience with consistent habits. While challenges inflict temporary pain, they also contain hidden growth opportunities. By leaning into trials with courage, we build the profound strength to thrive in darkness and light. You already contain that power within. Unleash your resilience.

# Chapter 3: Taming Your Inner Critic

We all have an inner voice that judges our perceived flaws, failures, and inadequacies - this is the inner critic. While intended to protect us, the critic often undermines self-confidence with excessive criticism. Left unchecked, it fuels anxiety and self-doubt. By identifying core critical messages and cultivating self-compassion, we can tame this overactive inner voice.

This chapter explores common forms the inner critic assumes and how to recognize when it is active. You will gain strategies for muzzling the critic, balancing its harshness with kindness. By asserting control over your self-talk, you can override the critic's distortions and finally make peace with yourself.

## What is the Inner Critic?

The inner critic is the part of our psyche that scrutinises our perceived imperfections and errors. It generates an inner monologue of rebuke to highlight flaws and mistakes. Everyone has a critic, as it evolves to promote self-improvement and social acceptance by preventing actions that may incur judgement.

However, in many, the critic is hyperactive, spewing excessive criticism that fuels anxiety and self-doubt. The critic's nagging voice magnifies normal failures into proofs of inadequacy. Perceived flaws get exaggerated beyond reality.

**Common inner critic messages include:**

- "You're so stupid for messing up."

- "Nobody actually likes you."

- "You're such a failure."

- "You're worthless."

- "You'll never amount to anything."

When such harsh judgments run through our minds repeatedly, they mould how we see ourselves. Over time, chronic self-criticism manifests as:

- Perfectionism

- Hyper-sensitivity to mistakes

- Extreme defensiveness and denial of flaws

- Catastrophizing minor setbacks

- Imposter syndrome and lack of self-worth


Learning to recognize when your inner critic is active is the first step in developing healthier self-talk patterns. Catching criticisms early prevents them from spiralling.

**Identifying Your Inner Critic**

Since everyone's inner critic is a bit different, tuning in to identify your personal critic's characteristics and common complaints is illuminating. Here are some ways to get acquainted with your critic.

-        Notice when your confidence suddenly drops or anxiety spikes. Ask yourself what self-critical thought triggered the change in state.

-        Think back to upsetting past experiences. What cruel self-talk did you engage in before, during or after?

-        Pay attention to the tone you use toward yourself. Would you talk that way to a dear friend? If not, that's the critic.

-        Examine the types of events that activate your inner monologue of self-judgment. This reveals sensitivities.

-        Journal out your inner chatter during stressful times. Unfiltered writing exposes critic themes.

-        Share examples of your self-talk with a trusted therapist or friend. An outsider's perspective helps reveal distortions.


With awareness, patterns surface around when your inner critic derides you and what specifically it targets. Once familiar with these cues, you can swiftly spot critic attacks and implement constructive responses before destructive self-talk escalates.

**Ways to Silence Your Inner Critic**

Once adept at noticing when your inner critic is active, you can experiment with strategies to muzzle its disparaging narrative and replace criticisms with compassion. Here are techniques to try:

-        **Label** - Name the inner voice as your critic to create distance from it. "This is just my overactive inner critic talking."

-        **Collect evidence** – Challenge criticisms by gathering factual examples that disprove them. Treat it like a debate.

-        **Get an outside opinion** – Ask a trusted friend if the critic's claims match reality. Outside input defuses distortions.

-        **Talk to your critic** – Have an inner dialogue addressing your critic's concerns calmly. Thank it for the input but set boundaries.

-        **Visualise muzzling your critic** – Imagine placing duct tape over your critic's mouth or locking it in a cage. Have fun with it!

-        **Interrupt the pattern** – Sing a song, call a friend or engage in an activity that forces your inner chatter to stop.

-        **Practise self-compassion** – Counter every criticism with a kind, rational statement. Balance negative self-talk.

The goal is not to banish your inner critic completely, as it serves a purpose in preventing faux pas. Instead, monitor its disproportionate negativity and intervene with logic and compassion to gain control over your inner dialogue. In time, self-talk naturally converts to be more balanced, fair and focused on growth.

## Why We Criticise Ourselves

To make peace with our inner critic, it is helpful to understand why it exists. The inner critic arises in childhood as we internalise criticism from parents, teachers, peers and society. We adopt negative self-talk to avoid external scolding and achieve goals faster via pressure.

However, this learned self-judgement often continues unchecked into adulthood and manifests as:

-       Perfectionism – We feel we must live up to sky-high standards or face criticism. The fear of disappointing others haunts us.

-       Imposter syndrome – Despite achievements, we feel secretly inadequate compared to peers. Accolades never seem deserved.

-       Hyper-sensitivity – We excessively dread others' disapproval or rejection. Every criticism cuts deeply even when minor.

-       Self-punishment – We beat ourselves up over failures and shortcomings instead of practising self-forgiveness and patience.

The inner critic aims to protect us from shame by ensuring we avoid mistakes, conceal flaws and meet expectations. However, its execution typically backfires, undermining our confidence and capacity for joy.

By realising this, we empower ourselves to break free of the perfectionist mind-set and meet setbacks with self-compassion, not self-recrimination. We are worthy of love exactly as we are, imperfections and all.

## Developing Self-Compassion

The counterbalance to excessive self-criticism is selfcompassion - treating ourselves kindly, as we would a dear friend. Research shows self-compassion strongly correlates with mental health and resilience while muting the inner critic. We must replace self-judgement with regular doses of understanding and care.

## Ways to strengthen self-compassion include:

-       Offer encouragement to yourself, as you would another in your situation. Validate your efforts.

-       Avoid harshly judging yourself for normal mistakes and flaws. Talk to yourself as a loving parent or mentor would.

-       Be mindfully aware of when you fall into self-criticism and intentionally shift to compassion and reason.

-       Treat yourself to small pleasures that lift your spirit - relaxing baths, nature walks, favourite foods.

-       Speak kindly to yourself out loud. Vocal reassurances feel more powerful when heard.

-       Write a letter of support to yourself as if from your wisest, most compassionate friend. Keep it to reread later.

-       Identify self-critical beliefs that stem from childhood experience or trauma and consciously release them. They no longer serve you.

-       Immerse yourself in supportive communities who validate your worth, so it emanates from within.

With consistent effort, compassion gradually transforms your inner dialogue and relationships. The judgments directed inward begin flowing outward as patience and understanding. By befriending yourself fully, self-acceptance radiates.


**In Summary**

The inner critic's constant commentary generates much psychological suffering. However, by identifying its voice and patterns, we can gain awareness and practice strategies to temper its distortions. When we counter criticism with compassion, our perspective expands to acknowledge that all humans are imperfect - and worthy of love regardless. Therein lies the path to self-acceptance, along with the grace to extend the same compassion to others as they walk their own imperfect journeys. Our inner light awaits. 8

# Chapter 4: Boosting Self-Esteem

Self-esteem is defined as our overall subjective evaluation of our own worth and capabilities. Those with healthy self-esteem trust in their value, effectively manage challenges, and have positive self-regard. In contrast, low self-esteem manifests as excessive self-criticism, perfectionism, and negative self perceptions. Fortunately, with intention and practice, self-esteem can be strengthened.

This chapter explores the psychological bases of self-esteem and how it is shaped in childhood. You will gain insight on how to identify and reframe negative core beliefs while celebrating positive attributes and practising holistic self-care. As we dismantle distortions and treat ourselves with greater kindness, self-esteem gradually grows. The journey toward self acceptance begins within.

## The Psychology of Self-Esteem

According to humanistic psychologist Carl Rogers, self-esteem arises from the alignment between our actual selves and our ideal selves. The actual self is who we are, while the ideal self represents who we think we should be. The closer self-perception matches our ideals, the greater our self-esteem. However, when a wide gap exists between the two, self-esteem suffers.

The origins of our self-concept begin in early childhood based on treatment from parents and other influential figures.

Feedback suggesting our value is contingent upon meeting specific standards breeds an unstable sense of self-worth. However, with care and introspection, these scripts can be rewritten.

**Hallmarks of healthy self-esteem include:**

- Accurately acknowledging your strengths and limitations

- Recognizing your inherent worth independent of achievements

- Handling criticism and setbacks with resilience

- Pursuing fulfilment aligned with your values

- Possessing inner confidence and self-compassion

- Feeling comfortable socially and asking for needs to be met

- Seeing value in your unique personality and perspective

The journey toward higher self-esteem involves dismantling the notion that worth derives from perfect behaviour. Our shared identity as imperfect but worthy human beings remain unchanged by the passing struggles. With compassionate self-reflection, we can realise our wholeness.

**Identifying Core Beliefs**

Our subjective self-impressions stem from a network of beliefs we hold about ourselves, others and the world. Some of these are generated in childhood and impact our self-esteem unconsciously. Bringing them into awareness is key.

**Commonly held distortions include:**

- I am inadequate compared to others.

- I am unlovable because I'm different.

- I am a failure if I make mistakes.

- My value depends on pleasing others.

- I must be perfect to earn love/praise.

Start by noting times when you feel particularly insecure or self-critical. Then examine your self-talk in those moments to identify underlying core beliefs. Uncover embedded rules you try to live by:

- What perceived flaws or shortcomings cause you the most shame?

- When do you feel urged to meet impossibly high standards?

- What basic beliefs about yourself do you take for granted as true?

- How did key figures and experiences in your past shape these?

- How are you internally punished when you violate these rules?

Gaining awareness of self-limiting core beliefs, we implicitly abide by allows us to dismantle their power. We can challenge their irrational basis and detach self-worth from their required standards.

## Reframing Negative Core Beliefs

Once core beliefs have been brought to light, we can begin reframing their distortions and loosening their grasp on our self-esteem.

## For each negative core belief, ask yourself:

- Is this 100% true all the time or an overgeneralization? What are exceptions?

- How would you respond to a loved one who held this belief about themselves? Does it stem from self-compassion or self-criticism?

- What evidence disproves this as an absolute truth? What nuance exists?

- How would this belief need to change to align with reality?

- What resonates as a more balanced and self-loving alternative?

For example, if you believe "I am a failure if I make any mistakes", interrogate this:

- Perfectionism is unrealistic. Everyone makes mistakes sometimes, even highly successful people. This belief lacks nuance.

- I would reassure a loved one in this situation rather than judge them. My own self-talk should reflect the same compassion.

- I have succeeded in many areas, even if imperfectly. My worth remains, regardless of occasional errors.

- Failure in one specific situation does not define my entire life. I choose to define myself holistically.

- A kinder statement could be "I learn from my mistakes, but they do not wholly diminish my value or capabilities."

Adjust core beliefs into affirmations resonating as realistic and loving. Repeat these aloud when old distortions resurface until new neural pathways form. Be patient with yourself in this gradual process.

### Celebrating Strengths

To heal the gap between your actual and ideal selves, celebrate qualities and accomplishments that exemplify your best self. This balances perfectionistic fixations on flaws. Reflect on times when you demonstrated:

Creativity - What inspired ideas have you brought to life?

- Curiosity - What topics energise your sense of wonder?

- Courage - When have you stepped outside your comfort zone?

- Compassion - How have you supported others in difficult times?

- Humour - What makes you smile and laugh each day?

- Resilience - How have you overcome setbacks and loss?

- Kindness - When have you brightened someone's day with a gesture of care?

- Resourcefulness - What solutions have you improvised?

- Dedication - What goals required focused effort over time?

- Principled living - How do you aim to contribute good to the world?

Keep an ongoing list of your strengths, talents, and values evident in your life. Add to it regularly with each new accomplishment and milestone. Read this when you need reminding that you are so much more than your failures. Your worth transcends checking boxes; it is woven into your essence.

## Self-Esteem Through Self-Care

Any journey of improved self-esteem requires holistic self-care. Research confirms activities like exercise, healthy eating, restorative sleep, creativity, time in nature and mindfulness all

correlate with higher self-esteem. By consistently nourishing your whole being, you reinforce your inherent value.

**Explore integrating self-care routines such as:**

- Daily movement - yoga, walking, dance

- Preparing healthy, nourishing meals

- Setting regular sleep hours and relaxing bedtime rituals

- Establishing tech-free zones - especially the bedroom

- Expressing yourself creatively through art, music, writing

- Immersing in nature and spending time with animals

- Making time for deep breathing, meditation, prayer

- Doing calming activities before bed - reading, stretching

- Surrounding yourself with positive, supportive people

- Speaking kindly to yourself with encouragement

- Keeping a gratitude journal to reflect on blessings

When you consistently care for your health and soul, self-doubt

loses its foothold. You cannot feel unworthy while simultaneously nourishing your whole being with love.

**In Summary**

Low self-esteem results from distorted core beliefs of deficiency reinforced over time. However, by identifying these beliefs and challenging their basis in reality we can gradually replace self-limiting narratives with compassionate truths. We enhance this process further through celebrating our strengths, practising holistic self-care, and treasuring ourselves unconditionally. You are worthy of love, joy and fulfilment exactly as you are in this moment. May this journey of self-discovery fill you with the freedom of self-acceptance. You contain such beauty, and you always have. It is time now to fully witness your light.

# Chapter 5: Mastering Time Management

Time is our most precious and limited resource. How we choose to spend it shapes our productivity, stress levels, and overall wellbeing. Time management is the process of organising and planning how to divide your time between specific tasks and goals. Mastering it leads to greater efficiency, less frustration, and increased life satisfaction.

This chapter provides strategies for auditing how you currently spend time, identifying core priorities, overcoming procrastination, and scheduling your days intentionally. Implementing effective time management habits frees you from feeling overwhelmed so you can channel focus toward meaningful priorities. Reclaim control of your time to create a life aligned with your deepest values.

### Assessing Current Use of Time

The first step in improving time management is assessing how you currently spend your hours. Are you investing time in alignment with your goals and values? Or does the day slip away, reacting, yet feeling unfulfilled?

Dedicate a week to completing a detailed time audit tracking all activities and time spent. Note:

- Main work tasks and time on each

- Household errands and chores

- Family, friend and relationship time

Entertainment like TV, internet, gaming

- Self-care like exercise, cooking, reading

- Miscellaneous appointments and obligations

Tally how you use your finite time during an average week. Where do you spend the majority? Are you content with this breakdown? What changes would better align time use with your priorities?

A time audit illuminates where you devote your most precious resource and whether you feel that investment was worthwhile. This establishes a benchmark for improving time allocation moving forward.

## Identifying Core Priorities

With insight from your time audit, reflect on your core values and goals to identify top priorities for investment moving forward. Common spheres of focus include: - Career – progress and fulfilment

- Relationships – nurturing connections

- Physical health – exercise, nutrition, check-ups

- Mental wellbeing – stress management, self-care

- Spiritual growth – practices nourishing the soul

- Finances – earning, saving, budgeting wisely

- Contribution – community service, volunteer work

- Learning and creativity – gaining knowledge, expressing yourself

**To narrow these to top priorities, ask:**

- If I could only focus on one area over the next 3-6 months, what matters most? Why?

- Where do I feel I am neglecting key priorities lately in my schedule?

- What current activities or responsibilities feel misaligned with my core goals?

Defining 2-4 top priorities channels proactive time management toward your highest aims. All decisions about investing time moving forward get evaluated against these essential goals. Activities receiving little return should get minimised or cut.

**Conquering Procrastination**

Procrastination is consistently rated as a top obstacle hindering productivity and fuelling regret over poor time management. It traps us in guilt cycles yet feels irresistible. Underlying reasons for procrastination typically include:

- Feeling overwhelmed by complexity or scope of tasks

- Perfectionism and fear of failure causing avoidance

Lacking clarity on goals, next steps or confidence in our abilities

- Self-sabotage and struggling with self-discipline

- Immediate gratification from easier distractions hijacking focus

Thankfully, behavioural psychology offers several strategies to conquer debilitating procrastination:

1. Break large tasks into bite-sized next steps with clearly defined completion points.

2. Set a timer for short intervals (25-45 minutes) and race against the clock.

3. Reward yourself after completing each step or session.

4. Remove distractions and create optimal conditions for focus.

5. Communicate deadlines to others for accountability.

6. Notice self-sabotaging thoughts and consciously redirect to task.

7. Forgive yourself for imperfections. Progress trumps perfection.

As momentum builds, tasks feel increasingly achievable. Splitting work into defined segments provides structure while offering a frequent sense of accomplishment as you tick off completed pieces. Consistency compounds over time.

## Scheduling Tips and Tricks

Even with the best intentions, days slip away without intentional time management. Thoughtfully scheduling priorities into your calendar ensures you actually invest time on what matters rather than reacting.

**Helpful strategies include:**

- Block schedule set times for core priorities like exercise, family, passion projects. Treat them as seriously as work meetings.

- Batch similar tasks like phone calls to minimise switching time between roles.

- Schedule tasks requiring deep focus early when energy is best. Fill afternoons with lighter items.

- Limit scheduling only 4-5 key priorities daily to keep load realistic.

- Identify peak productive hours and protect them for big projects.

- Use weekends to plan the week ahead and get organised.

- Set alerts on your calendar 15 minutes before appointments as a reminder to transition focus.

- Schedule breaks every 90 minutes for mental recharge and recovery.

End each workday by planning tomorrow. Review priorities and to-do list.

- Maintain a master long-term calendar with key dates like trips and program deadlines for proactive planning.

While scheduling seems rigid, built-in flexibility remains vital. Leave buffer time for the unexpected. Also, regularly reevaluate priorities and time allocation as personal and work demands evolve. Maintain an agile schedule aligned with your most pressing present goals.

**Maximising Productivity**

In addition to scheduling intentionally, adopting key practices maximises productivity with existing time:

- Keep a running task list organised by priority. Review it before starting work.

- Eliminate unnecessary meetings and phone calls. Request agenda and desired outcomes beforehand.

- Decline or delegate tasks that detract from core priorities. Learn to say no.

- Master the 80/20 rule. 80% of output comes from 20% of activities. Focus where you add most value.

- Minimise distractions like email, messaging and internet surfing.

-        Recharge productivity by exercising, snacking, or changing scenery when energy crashes.

-        Work in focused 60–90-minute sprints between breaks rather than endless hours. Intensity trumps length.

-        Multitask carefully. Limit to simple repetitive tasks. Most cognitively complex work requires full attention.

By honouring your natural rhythms while implementing time boxes and productivity best practices, you achieve more in less time. Focus on applying consistent energy in the right direction.

Time Management Tools and Technology

From old-fashioned paper planners to new apps, myriad tools exist to support time management. Find systems that easily integrate into your natural flow.

**Helpful options include:**

-        Calendar apps syncing across devices with reminders and organisation features.

-        Paper planners and bullet journals with space for task lists and notes

-        Digital or paper to-do list apps for capturing tasks and prioritising by urgency/importance

-        Timer apps for tracking work and break sessions or intervals when focused

Noise-cancelling headphones or apps with ambient sounds to reduce distraction

-       Collaboration apps for delegating, scheduling meetings, and tracking project progress

-       Note taking apps for outlining goals, next steps and big picture project plans

Experiment to find technology that streamlines rather than overcomplicates. The best systems require minimal effort to maintain daily. Select tools aligning with your organisational style.


**In Summary**

Our fast-paced, task-saturated world leaves many feelings scattered and overwhelmed by poor time management. Yet by carefully auditing how we spend finite time and thoughtfully scheduling aligned with values, transformational focus becomes possible. Implementing productivity best practices and tools creates order from chaos. With intention, align the hours of your precious life with who and what matters most. There is no greater opportunity or responsibility than stewarding well your limited time. Make each moment count.

# Chapter 6: Decluttering Your Life

Clutter is defined as an excessive number of possessions, obligations and information that creates overwhelmedness and stress. Physical clutter makes spaces feel chaotic. Digital clutter overwhelms with notifications and data. Mental clutter arises from trying to juggle too many responsibilities or ideas simultaneously. Decluttering is the act of sorting through excess to pare life down to essentials.

This chapter explores the psychological research on how clutter harms wellbeing and productivity. You will gain strategies for decluttering physical spaces, digital devices, and calendars through assessing wants versus needs, establishing systems, and embracing simplicity. By purging superfluities, you gain freedom to focus on what truly matters.

## The Costs of Clutter

While occasionally dismissed as merely an organisational nuisance, studies reveal clutter exacts real psychological and physiological tolls by:

- Increasing stress hormones like cortisol

- Impairing concentration and mental clarity

- Draining energy through constant low-level visual cacophony

- Reducing productivity and efficiency

- Creating feelings of anxiety and being overwhelmed
  Sabotaging sleep quality when bedrooms are disorderly

- Triggering conflicts due to lost objects and frustration

Additionally, an overabundance of possessions feeds clutter by promoting:

- Attachment to objects for security versus inner sources

- Materialism and basing self-worth on stuff rather than character

- Compulsive shopping to fill voids better addressed otherwise

- Sentimental holding onto gifts, inherited items, or memorabilia beyond usefulness or reason

- Acquisition of unnecessary trinkets and duplicates  - Buying

  storage solutions versus eliminating root excess

Clutter thrives when we seek outer Band-Aids for inner unrest. Sustainable decluttering works from the inside out, aligning possessions with authentic needs.


**Assessing Clutter**

To begin, conduct a thorough clutter assessment. Walk through each area of your home, office and digital spaces answering:

- How does this space make me feel – calm or chaos?

- What percentage of items here do I regularly use?

- What duplicates, unused items or broken things exist here?

What have I stored just because it was free or a gift?

- What truly sparks joy or eases daily life in this space?

- What excess information exists here? When did I last review it?

- What tasks or ideas feel overwhelming to manage here?

- What could I remove today with no loss to my life?

Similar audits of inboxes, subscriptions, bookmarks and devices reveal overaccumulation. Be ruthlessly honest. Any denial or avoidance reflects attachment. The goal is eliminating distractions and barriers to efficiency. Surplus possession of any type drains life energy.

**Establishing Daily Systems**

With clutter assessed, establish basic daily systems to maintain order. For example:

-        Never place anything down without a designated "home" for it to return.

-        Process mail immediately, recycling junk and responding promptly.

- Follow the "one in, one out" rule for new belongings – hemming accumulation.

  Schedule a daily tidy of high traffic areas like entryways, kitchens, and offices.

- End each day by tidying completely – clothes put away, dishes done, surfaces cleared.

- Develop consistent digital file systems on computers for locating documents easily.

- Unsubscribe instantly from emails that no longer interest you. Curate inboxes.

- Sort physical paper into "action" and "reference" files. Toss when obsolete.

- Backup digital data regularly and delete device files not needed long-term.

Daily habits prevent escalation of disorder. Consistency maintains functionality and cleanliness better than occasional purges when systems are lacking.


## Decluttering Physical Spaces

For more embedded physical clutter, use these strategies room-by-room:

**Kitchens and Pantries:**

- Toss expired foods and donate unopened extras to food banks.

  Organise supplies efficiently - containers to corral loose items.

- If you cannot comfortably visualise the contents, the space needs decluttering.

**Bedrooms:**

- Remove unused furniture crowding the room.

- Designate boxes or closets for out of season clothes storage to open space.

- Keep only essentials like lamps, alarm, and water beside bed. Reduce visual noise.

- Make closet floors visible. Use vertical space on rods. Discard what no longer fits.

**Bathrooms:**

- Toss expired medications and dried up cosmetics.

- Store bathroom linens neatly within cabinets, not piled everywhere.

- Use trays and bins to segregate supplies in drawers.

**Garage and Basements**:

- Designate zones for tools, seasonal items, sports equipment. Label shelves.

  Hold a garage sale to profit from unused equipment and furniture.

- Recycle or donate any building supplies leftover from completed projects.

- Schedule pickup for larger unneeded furniture pieces.


**Office and Paperwork:**

- File paperwork immediately or recycle it.

- Unsubscribe from catalogues and junk mail lists to reduce incoming paper.

- Scan documents for digital archiving then shred originals when possible.

- Clear surfaces completely except essential office supplies and devices.

When decluttering, discard first, then organise remaining items efficiently. Be merciless. If not used in years, it is unlikely to improve your life going forward.

## Decluttering Digital Spaces

Emails, notifications, bookmarks, downloads, and files clutter digital space, demanding attention and diverting focus. Apply the 80/20 rule - 80% of online activity concentrates around 20% of our favourite sites and apps. To reclaim cognitive bandwidth:

-       Unsubscribing from non-vital email lists. Delete accounts you do not regularly use.

-       Clear browser bookmarks except essential 20%. Revisit old ones to delete if obsolete.

-       Mute notifications from apps not crucial to daily work and wellbeing.

-       Delete downloads and files no longer needed. Back up important data to external drives.

-       Reset devices to factory settings to clear bloatware and refresh speed.

-       Consolidate multi-device photos to main storage then delete device duplicates.

-       Cancel dormant streaming, subscription, and social media accounts draining finances and time.

By curating your digital ecosystem around your core needs, productivity and satisfaction increase. Avoid accumulating new apps, accounts, and downloads without an ongoing purpose. Digital minimalism restores attention and control.

## Decluttering Obligations

Beyond physical possessions and digital data, our time gets cluttered when we overcommit obligations and activities. The resulting stress fuels anxiety and exhaustion when demands exceed resources. Preserve mental clarity and calm by:

-        Keeping a running list of obligations with deadlines. Remove completed items promptly.

-        Setting firm boundaries around your availability — limit what you take on.

-        Delegating or outsourcing tasks that are not essential priorities.

-        Checking calendars and agendas before agreeing to additional requests. Decline politely if your plate is already full.

-        Ending memberships/subscriptions no longer served by. Assess if the value received merits the cost.

-        Reducing extracurriculars if stretched thin. Better to do a few things well than overload life.

Give responsibilities the consistent time and focus they deserve by eliminating clutter competing for attention. Do not overwhelm your schedule to the point quality and self-care get sacrificed.

## Embracing Simplicity

In addition to initial decluttering sessions, intentionally embracing simplicity long-term prevents accumulation and clutter from returning. Some suggestions:

-        Before acquiring new possessions, ask yourself if they align with your values and fill a genuine (not impulsive) need.

-        When considering new opportunities and obligations, evaluate if they support your core priorities before agreeing. Just because something is good does not mean it fits in your life presently.

-        Highlight activities and relationships nourishing your soul. Invest in those rather than chasing recognition or social comparison.

-        Cherish quality experiences over quantity of possessions and busywork.

-        Eat simply, dress modestly, and carry little. Embrace minimalism as a lifestyle.

-        Unplug regularly for set times to immerse in nature, loved ones, and your inner world apart from screens and noise.

The deepest joys in life are free - time with loved ones, laughter, learning, experiencing nature and culture. Structure your days around simplicity to regularly reconnect with what matters most.

**In Summary**

Clutter's constant visual noise subtly but meaningfully harms our wellbeing - disrupting concentration, raising stress, and complicating life. While decluttering requires initial time investment, the lasting benefits of order and efficiency liberate precious mental bandwidth. By consciously eliminating excess possessions, digital data, and obligations through daily systems and embracing simplicity, we focus on our highest priorities with clarity and calm. Intentional living guided by core values emerges.

# Chapter 7: Sleeping Deeply

Sleep is profoundly vital for physical and mental health, yet many struggle with insufficient or low-quality rest. Understanding sleep neuroscience reveals how to harness its full restorative potential through optimising sleep routines, environment and habits. This chapter explores creating an oasis for sleep emphasising releasing the day's tensions, establishing restful pre-bed wind down rituals, and keeping bedrooms cool, dark and technology free. Implementing healthy sleep hygiene reduces insomnia, boosts daytime productivity, and restores the body's innate rhythms. Discover the pathway to sleeping deeply tonight and waking refreshed.

## The Science of Sleep Needs

Despite occupying one-third of life, sleep remains mysterious. Research continues illuminating its critical functions for learning, emotional regulation, immune health, neurological housekeeping and more. Deficiencies impair all aspects of wellbeing.

Adults require 7-9 hours nightly for optimal performance. Yet studies reveal 1 in 3 adults fall short of this, with detrimental effects compounding over time. Lost sleep cannot be recovered later, highlighting the need for consistent healthy sleep.

**Sleep falls into two primary categories:**

Non-REM (quiet) sleep initiates sleep cycles through progressively deeper stages (1-3) of light to slow wave sleep. Blood pressure lowers, muscles relax, tissue growth and repair occur, and memories consolidate during these phases. You spend about 75% of overall sleep in non-REM.

REM (rapid eye movement) sleep follows non-REM cycles every 90 minutes, comprising 25% of total sleep. Brain wave frequency increases, eyes dart rapidly and dreaming occurs. REM sleep supports emotional regulation, procedural learning, and daytime alertness. REM particularly increases before waking to rouse the mind gently.

Both non-REM and REM sleep perform indispensable biological functions. Overall sleep quality involves transitioning smoothly through all sleep stages multiple times nightly. Disruptions to this natural cycle prevent restorative sleep.

## Common Causes of Sleep Disruption

A constellation of harmful habits disrupts healthy sleep patterns. The most prevalent include: - Irregular sleep hours and bedtimes

- Light and noise pollution in bedrooms

- Stimulant use (caffeine, alcohol, drugs) before bed

- Heavy, late-night meals upsetting digestion

- Using phones, laptops and TVs before bedtime

- Unmanaged stress and anxiety

- Underlying health issues like sleep apnoea or chronic pain

- Medications that act as stimulants

Modifying sleep hygiene offers safer, sustainable solutions to insomnia than long-term medication dependence. Set yourself up for success by curating bedrooms and pre-bed routines catering to calm and relief from the day's tensions. The mind naturally settles when conditions align.

**Creating an Optimal Sleep Environment**

Design bedrooms expressly for sanctuary and slumber. Keep the following guidelines in mind:

**Furniture:**

- Invest in a high-quality mattress ensuring comfort and support. Replace old mattresses regularly as materials compress.

- Use comfortable, non-distracting bedding - soft, breathable sheets and lightweight blankets that maintain comfort through the night.

- Position the bed away from windows to reduce light interference.

**Technology and Lighting:**

- Eliminate all blue light-emitting screens like TVs, phones and computers from the bedroom. The suppression of natural melatonin ruins sleep.

- Install room-darkening shades or a sleep mask to block external light pollution. Complete darkness increases deep sleep.

- Set adjustable warm lighting to dim gradually before bedtime, signalling the brain to release melatonin.


**Temperature and Sound:**

- Cooler ambient temperatures around 65 Fahrenheit facilitate sleeping. Keep blankets light enough to prevent overheating.

- Consider a white noise machine or fan to establish consistent background noise blocking disruptions. Ear plugs also work.

- Use a humidifier if dry air causes congestion and disruption.

Only rest-promoting items should occupy the sleep sanctuary. If children or pets disturb the bedroom, create spaces nearby where they can rest undisturbed. Defending sleep time consistently trains the brain toward release and restoration.

## Cultivating a Pre-Sleep Routine

How you spend the 90 minutes before bedtime greatly impacts sleep readiness. Harness pre-bedtime routines to release the day's mental tension and ease into rest. Essential steps include:

- Establish a consistent bedtime allowing for adequate sleep hours. Follow this schedule, even on weekends.

- Dim lights incrementally 1-2 hours before bedtime to increase melatonin secretion.

- Avoid caffeine, alcohol, heavy foods and exercise 3-4 hours before bedtime.

- Take a warm bath or shower to relax muscles and lower body temperature.

- Power down digital devices and screens. Read books or write instead.

- Spend time reflecting on gratitude, hopes for tomorrow, or affirmations.

- Practise deep breathing, meditation or light yoga sequences to calm the nervous system.

- Stretch gently or receive a massage to loosen muscles and reduce physical tension.

- Listen to soothing music or nature sounds.

Repeating these rituals cues the mind-body that bedtime approaches. Consistency builds associations between activities and subsequent sleepiness. Nightly dedication bears fruitful rest.


## Optimising Sleep Habits

In addition to bedrooms and pre-bed routines, daily lifestyle habits dramatically impact nightly rest:

-        Rise and sleep at consistent times, even on weekends. Regularity entrains circadian rhythms.

-        Spend time outdoors in natural daylight, especially mornings. Sunlight and fresh air boost energy through the day.

-        Exercise daily, but not right before bedtime. Aerobic movement deepens sleep.

-        Limit stimulating substances like caffeine, nicotine and sugar in the afternoons and evenings.

-        Manage stress effectively through meditation, journaling, therapy and calming hobbies. Anxiety disrupts sleep.

-        Take brief 20-minute power naps as needed but limit them to prevent interference with nighttime sleep.

-        Eat whole foods and avoid heavy meals near bedtime that tax digestion.

Ongoing lifestyle tweaks generate compounding gains, optimising sleep long-term. Remember that consistency carves new grooves yielding exponential change over time.

## In Summary

Sleep is the bedrock of physical vitality and mental clarity. By intentionally designing optimised bedrooms, establishing unwinding rituals in the evening, and integrating healthy lifestyle habits daily, high-quality sleep becomes possible for everyone. Follow your body's innate rhythms. Prioritise sleep without guilt and witness the remarkable gains in your daytime productivity, mood and sense of wellbeing. Happy dreaming!

# Chapter 8: Eating for Energy and Health

Food is the fuel powering our days. Consciously crafting eating patterns centred on nourishing whole foods dramatically uplifts physical vitality, reduces disease risks, stabilises mood and sharpens mental clarity. However, amidst busy schedules and endless diet messaging, intuitively eating well often falls by the wayside.

This chapter explores mindful eating, evidence-based nutrition guidelines, meal planning strategies and quick stress-reducing snacks. By returning to simpler, more intuitive eating guided by your body's wisdom, you can elevate energy levels, lower inflammation and feel your best every day. Foods delightful in both taste and nutrition abound.

### The Benefits of Mindful Eating

Mindful eating means choosing meals around full sensory awareness and connection. This contrasts the common habit of distractedly eating in front of devices or computer screens while working. The principles include:

- Paying full attention to the process of eating - noticing texture, taste, smells and sounds

- Tuning into physical hunger cues directing when and how much to eat

Appreciating nourishment entering your body and the efforts of all involved in food journeys.

- Honouring your body's natural appetite and satiety signals

- Making deliberate, balanced food choices aligned with health goals

- Eliminating distractions like phones, screens and reading during mealtimes

Studies confirm mindful eating aids digestion, strengthens intuitive eating regulation, decreases impulsive food choices and reduces stress-linked binge eating. Slowing down helps appreciate flavours and nutritional value. Meals become meditative rituals nourishing the whole self.

## Intuitive Eating Principles

Intuitive eating complements mindful eating by emphasising following your body's innate cues guiding when, what and how much to eat. Regain sensitivity to your body's wisdom by:

- Eating when physically hungry, stopping when full - avoiding strict schedules

- Satisfying cravings in moderation - deprivation fuels bingeing

- Choosing foods that both taste delicious and nourish health

- Balancing lighter and heavier foods to feel energised yet stable

  Reflecting on how certain foods physically impact your wellbeing

- Avoiding labelling foods as "good" or "bad" since all have a place in balance.

- Examining emotional motivations behind wanting food

By directing attention both inward and toward your plate, intuitive eating reveals optimal fuelling patterns personalised for your body's needs and activity levels. Trust emerges as you honour natural hunger and fullness. No strict dieting required.


**Nutrition Fundamentals for Energy and Health**

While individual needs vary, core nutrition fundamentals based on robust research promote optimal wellbeing:

-        Emphasise whole, minimally processed foods over refined, heavily processed products. Real food nourishes bodies deeply.

-        Focus on abundant vegetables, fruits, whole grains, beans, lentils, nuts and seeds. These deliver antioxidants, fibre and essential micronutrients.

-        Moderate animal protein intake to balance needs and avoid excess saturated fats. Enjoy in modest portions.

- Choose healthy fats like avocados, olive oil, nuts and Omega-3 fatty fish to reduce inflammation.

Stay hydrated with 8 cups of water daily minimum to aid digestion, circulation and detoxification.

- Limit added sugars, refined grains and artificial ingredients that spike blood sugar and energy crashes.

- Satisfy between-meal hunger with fresh fruits, vegetables and nuts instead of empty calorie snacks.

Use this nutrition blueprint to guide grocery lists and cooking practices for supporting consistent, stable energy levels and wellness.


## Designing a Healthy Plate

When building individual meals, the healthy plate model ensures balanced nutrition:

- Fill half your plate with non-starchy vegetables for antioxidants, fibre. and hydration. Spinach, kale, broccoli, cauliflower, asparagus, mushrooms, tomatoes, peppers and more.

- One quarter with lean protein such as fish, poultry, eggs, lowfat dairy, beans or meatless alternatives if desired. This sustains energy between meals.

-        The remaining quarter with whole grains like quinoa, brown rice, oatmeal and Ezekiel bread that offer satisfying fibre and nutrients.

Add in healthy fats like avocado slices, olive oil, nuts and seeds to reduce inflammation and aid nutrient absorption.

-        Round out meals with fresh fruit and colourful salads. Their phytonutrients and antioxidants strengthen immunity.

Aiming for this balance between vegetables, lean proteins, whole grains and healthy fats ensures you derive full nutrition from meals while feeling light yet satiated.

## Meal Planning Strategies

Meal planning is one of the most powerful tools for consistently eating nourishing foods amidst busy weeks. It eases daily decisions about what to eat and allows grocery shopping aligned with planned recipes. Helpful tips include:

-        Sketch out weekly dinner ideas aligned with your health goals. Select 2-3 recipes to repeat with leftovers to save time.

-        Note needed breakfast and lunch ingredients each recipe requires. Build your grocery list accordingly.

-        Prepare hearty proteins like chicken, fish or plant-based alternatives for easy meal additions. Roast a sheet pan of veggies.

-        Chop vegetables and pre-portion ingredients for grab and go smoothies or bowls once your home.

  Stock up on healthy convenience items like washed greens, frozen fruits and veggies, canned beans and fish.

-        Schedule an hour or so each weekend for grocery shopping and prep ingredients like grains and dressings for streamlined cooking.

The initial planning effort saves ample time later when meals come together easily. You gain mental spaciousness knowing nourishing meals await without scrambling.


**Quick Stress-Reducing Nutrition Strategies**

During tense or exhausting times, we often slip into grabbing sugary, fried or heavily processed items in desperation. However simple snacks and ingredients offer a convenient nutritional safety net:

- The apple and peanut butter classic - Fibre and protein provide sustaining energy.

- Carrots and hummus - Veggies + protein.

- Yogurt with berries and granola - Protein, antioxidants and fibre.


- Avocado and nut butter toast for healthy fats, fibre and protein.

- Smoothies with greens, banana, nut butter and pea protein powder.

  Rice cakes or celery with nut butter and raisins.

- Half an avocado with lime juice and salt. Potassium aids stress resilience.

- Air popped popcorn sprinkled with nutritional yeast for protein and B vitamins.

Planning go-to items provides quick nourishment under duress while honouring your health. Stressful times magnify nutrition needs. With support, the body rebounds faster.


**In Summary**

Few acts of self-care wield more power than intentionally fuelling the body with nourishing whole foods. Meals centred on vegetables, fruits, lean proteins and whole grains uplift energy levels and mental clarity while reducing inflammation. By planning weekly menus, prepping ahead, and keeping stress buffering snacks on hand, consistent healthy eating becomes effortless. Each bite lays the foundation for whole being wellness. Here's to the journey of intuitive eating guided by your body's wisdom!

# Chapter 9: Moving Your Body

Regular physical activity is one of the most powerful ways to uplift energy, mood and overall, well-being. Yet amid busy schedules, many struggle to prioritise movement. This chapter

provides evidence-based guidance on recommended activity levels along with strategies to find enjoyable forms of exercise and overcome common obstacles to consistency like lack of motivation. By discovering modes of movement that resonate with you personally and establishing momentum, the benefits of improved fitness, reduced anxiety and greater vitality await.

## The Mental Health Benefits of Exercise

Beyond physical health gains, consistent exercise delivers remarkable benefits for mental health via multiple pathways:

-       Alleviates depression and anxiety symptoms by raising endorphins, serotonin and dopamine while lowering stress hormones like cortisol. Studies confirm reduced risk of depressive episodes and anxiety disorders.

-       Improves sleep quality. 30 minutes daily raises body temperature and deepens sleep.

-       Boosts self-esteem through experiencing capability, setting goals, and witnessing progress.

- Creates a sense of meaning, community and joy through group activities like sports, classes and walking with friends. Our brains are wired for connection.

- Enhances the growth of new neurons and neural connections to boost mood and learning capability. It literally expands the brain.

- Acts as moving mindfulness, fostering present moment focus and relief from rumination.

For optimal gains, studies point to 30-60 minutes of moderate intensity aerobic activity 4-5 days weekly plus 2 sessions of strength training. But some movement always beats none, so start wherever feels manageable.


**Recommended Types of Exercise**

Balance is key for sustained motivation and benefit. Aim to incorporate:

- Aerobic activity like walking, jogging, biking, swimming, dancing, sports - sustains stamina and burns calories. Shoot for raising the heart rate moderately for 30 consecutive minutes at least.


- Strength training using weights, resistance bands or bodyweight at least 2 days a week - builds muscle mass and strength for daily functioning.

-        Flexibility exercises like yoga, Pilates and stretching 2-3 days a week - enhances mobility and prevents injury, especially important as we age.

-        Short bursts of high intensity interval training (HIIT) intermittently - boosts metabolism, strength and endurance.

Experiment with modes you find fun and accessible to stick with long-term. Many activities provide hybrid benefits - for example, dancing builds stamina while improving coordination. Follow what feels joyful.

**Overcoming Exercise Barriers**

Despite proven benefits, only about 20% of adults accomplish recommended weekly exercise. Some top obstacles include:

Lack of motivation - Inspiration wanes over time. Counter by planning short periods (10-15 minutes) to begin so effort feels minimal. Celebrate completing any amount. Track progress.

Lack of time - Even 10 minutes activity several times daily counts. Schedule exercise like appointments. Wake up 30 minutes earlier.

Disliking exercise - Push past initial resistance for 5-10 minutes until the body warms up and releases endorphins. Pick an activity you once enjoyed as a child. Music boosts fun.

Inconvenience - Eliminate excuses by keeping equipment accessible - yoga mat by the TV, weights in living room, sneakers by door. Start small at home.

Physical discomfort - Move gently and respect limitations. Reduce high intensity. Stretch after warming up muscles. Proper footwear prevents pain.

Social awkwardness - Invite friends initially until comfortable attending classes alone. Some thrive on social interaction. Do what's best for you.

Forgive lapses. Consistency compounds over years through daily brief sessions. Note how much better you feel after moving versus remaining sedentary. Each time, you reinforce motivation circuits.

## Integrating Movement into Daily Routines

For time-pressed individuals, inserting spurts of activity into daily routines ensures regular movement:

## Morning:

- Wake up 30 minutes early to stretch, do yoga or walk outside energising the body and mind. The benefits linger for hours.

- After showering, perform a few strength exercises like planks, lunges and squats using just bodyweight.

- Dance to music as you get dressed and make breakfast.

**At Work:**

- Take the stairs whenever possible. Do calf raises if waiting for elevators.

- Stand during phone calls and walk around while talking.

- At lunch, walk outside or do desk exercises like shoulder rolls and marching in place.


**At Home:**

- Do squats, lunges or planks during TV show commercial breaks.

- Stretch as soon as home from work to unwind.

- Take relaxing evening walks with family or friends after dinner.

- Put on music and dance as you tidy up and get ready for bed.


Weave purposeful movement throughout all your hours. It quickly adds up and becomes habitual.


**Making Exercise Enjoyable**

To sustain motivation long-term, ensure exercise feels positively experiential rather than punitive. Strategies include:

-       Pick modes you find fun, energising and congruent with your values - tap into "play" versus "work" mentality. If bored, switch activities periodically.

-       Vary routines between solo and social activities. Interacting uplifts some individuals while others prefer introspection.

-       Infuse creativity into routines through dance, martial arts, adventure sports.

-       Exercise outdoors for boosts in mood and vitality. Natural environments inspire.

-       Listen to audiobooks or podcasts making solo workouts mentally engaging.

-       Set manageable targets allowing success experiences that reinforce self-efficacy. Avoid extreme difficulty causing discouragement. Progress from doable objectives.

-       Afterward, take 5-10 minutes to relax and appreciate how movement benefits your body and mind. Positive associations strengthen habits.

When exercise feels replenishing, you intuitively make time for it. Build in rewards like enjoying scenic nature, socialising, learning or playing music to deepen engagement.

**In Summary**

The health gains from regular aerobic, strength and flexibility exercise are clearly supported by extensive research. However, amid busy schedules, making movement a consistent habit remains elusive for many - exactly when it is needed most for reducing stress. By experimenting with enjoyable formats, integrating physical activity into daily life, and recognizing tangible improvements in energy, clarity and wellbeing motivation sustains. Your body inherently longs to move, play and be strong. By making time to listen, you tap into profound intuitive wisdom. Just take the first step.

# Chapter 10: Cultivating Connections

As humans, we are wired for connection. Research confirms that social ties strengthen mental and physical health, longevity, resilience to stress and overall life contentment. However, amidst busy modern life, these bonds frequently erode, leaving many feeling isolated and lonely. This chapter explores the foundations of friendship, romantic partnerships and community ties that leave us feeling seen, secure and valued. You will gain insights on deepening existing relationships along with strategies for combating loneliness by proactively reaching out. Our innate hunger for belonging awaits fulfilment.

## Why Relationships Matter

Both the quantity and quality of social connections shape wellbeing. Studies reveal close supportive relationships:

-        Reduce risks of anxiety, depression, addiction and suicidal thoughts by providing emotional stability. Therapy explores how relationship patterns affect mental health.

-        Improve cardiovascular health by lowering blood pressure and heart disease risks. Isolation conversely elevates disease and mortality rates.

-        Enhance immunity and speed healing as relationships help moderate stress hormone levels that suppress immune function if chronically elevated.

Support longevity, with research showing greater social integration linked to living longer lives, up to a 50% reduced mortality risk.

-       Provide meaning, purpose and a sense of community through sharing experiences with others. We thrive when feeling part of something larger than ourselves.

Actively nurturing relationships emerges as foundational for thriving across all life domains. Our brains evolved for networking. Investing in it deepens existing relationships

For current relationships, enrich connection through:

**Focused Quality Time**

-       Schedule regular one-on-one dates free of distractions like TV or phones. Be fully present.

-       Share activities you both enjoy - cooking, hiking, concerts. Novelty sparks bonding.

-       Ask thoughtful questions and reflectively listen without judgement.

-       Discuss dreams, hopes and values. Deeper sharing forges intimacy.

-

## Acts of Service

- Offer sincere compliments and praise character strengths.


- Surprise them with acts of kindness like bringing a favourite treat.

- Help with tasks or obligations important to them.

- Remember meaningful dates and milestones. Send reminders you are thinking of them.


## Shared Experiences

- Try new adventures together like museums, classes and cultural events.

- Go stargazing, camping, or explore nature, which inspires bonding.

- Volunteer together at places like animal shelters, community gardens and mentoring programs. Giving back fosters empathy and purpose.


## Barriers to Connection

- Avoid criticism and excessive venting, which breeds defensiveness and resentment. Focus on resolving issues, not complaining.

Don't take loved ones for granted. Regularly express appreciation.

- Honour each person's imperfections and changing needs over time. Accept them as human.

With core pillars like focused presence, service and fun novelty, relationships blossom. Remember, lasting bonds require consistent dedication, not grand sporadic gestures.

**Reaching Out to Combat Loneliness**

During periods of social isolation when existing relationships are unavailable, prioritise taking initiative to connect with new people. Warm communities abound when we step forward:

1.      Identify gaps in your social life in need of enrichment such as fun socialising, emotional support, purposeful volunteering or physical activity partners. Articulate the type of connections sought.

2.      Brainstorm settings and groups likely to attract like-minded individuals. Check out community centres, place of worship classes, hiking meetups, sports teams, book clubs.

3.      Attend several events to test compatibility. Focus on listening and learning about others. Practice vulnerability by opening up.

-

4.     Once finding potential kindred spirits, suggest meeting again. Offer contact info and follow through. Consistency builds familiarity.


5.     Express gratitude for new friendships. Thoughtfully consider ways to support others too through struggles. Reciprocity cements bonds.

Nurturing new seeds of friendship may feel vulnerable initially but blossoms connection where you need it most. Our fear of rejection often far exceeds reality. Give people a chance.


**Romantic Relationship Foundations**

For romantic partnerships, essential pillars to reinforce love include:

- Engaged listening and presence - avoiding distractions, giving full focus.

- Physical affection appropriate for the relationship - intimacy maintains the bond.

- Acts of practical service - helping with their tasks and needs.

- Shared fun, laughter and novel experiences - levity strengthens.

- Supporting their personal growth and dreams.

- Communicating admiration genuinely.

Keeping disagreements respectful, not belittling. Fair fighting principles protect the bond.

- Honouring alone time. Independence nurtures individual wellbeing.

- Assuming positive intent when frustrated. Perceived slights are often miscommunications, not malice.

- Willingness to seek help like therapy when communication falters. All relationships hit rough patches needing support.

With mutual dedication, relationships become our anchors. Invest time and care into these gardens. The fruits are sweet.


**In Summary**

The overriding takeaway is that our underlying longing for belonging resides deep in our DNA. Prioritising cultivating bonds with others - whether partners, family, friends or community - profoundly nurtures happiness and health. Schedule consistent relationship time as you would other obligations. Reach out instead of waiting passively for contacts. The rewards multiply exponentially in your life. As the saying goes, relationships are not just about finding the right people, but being the right people. Grow in friendship, generosity and compassion. Your whole world changes.

# Chapter 11: Practising Mindfulness

Mindfulness is defined as purposefully bringing full awareness to the present moment without judgement. Research confirms practising mindfulness reduces stress, sharpens focus, enriches relationships, boosts mood, and improves sleep and physical health. This chapter provides an overview of core mindfulness concepts and guided meditations, breathwork techniques, and habits for increasing present moment awareness amidst the distractions of daily responsibilities. By dedicating just a few minutes each day to tuning into sensory experiences, emotional landscapes, and the wisdom of the body, you tap into mindfulness as a grounding sanctuary.

## The Mindfulness Mind-set

Mindfulness is both a formal practice and an everyday mindset. At its core, it involves:

- Noticing thoughts, emotions and bodily sensations without attaching to them or letting them hijack attention

- Bringing full focus to whatever activity is in the present - washing dishes, walking, brushing teeth without multitasking

- Observing passing experiences with compassionate detachment rather than judgement

- Listening to intuitive wisdom gently arising amidst external noise

- Pausing before reacting to re-centre inner calm

In essence, mindfulness creates space around experiences, so they do not overwhelm. By consistently returning attention to the present, we realise our whole experience is continually evolving. Even painful emotions shift when observed with care. Mindfulness lets life unfold instead of frantically chasing fulfilment. Suffering diminishes.

## Benefits of Mindfulness

Extensive research reveals practising mindfulness delivers remarkable benefits:

- Lowers blood pressure, heart rate and stress hormone levels to reverse damage from chronic stress

- Reduces depression, anxiety and pain levels

- Improves focus and memory retention

- Strengthens relationship quality by increasing emotional presence

- Helps curb impulsive, addictive and binge behaviours

- Increases perceived energy levels and joy in daily activities

- Boosts sleep quality and physical immunity


- Cultivates self-compassion, helping tame inner critics

The more we infuse mindfulness into everyday life, the greater the gains. Even 5-10 minutes daily meditation makes a difference long-term.

## Establishing a Formal Practice

Formal mindfulness practice involves setting aside dedicated time for activities like breathwork, body scans, and open awareness meditation. Try starting with 5-10 minutes daily, then gradually increase duration to 20-45 minutes for optimal effect. Consistency matters most. Follow these guidelines:

- Find a quiet space where you can sit undisturbed without distractions or screens.

- Set a calming intention like openness, peace or joy. Release the need for specific outcomes.

- Sit comfortably with a tall, dignified posture to facilitate focus and energy flow. Close eyes or gaze softly downward.

- Begin with a few deep belly breaths. Inhale fully, exhaling out stress and tension.

- Bring attention to the physical sensations of breathing. Follow the breath moving in and out. Mind wandering is normal; gently return focus whenever it drifts.

- When finished, sit for a minute feeling the effects before transitioning back to daily tasks.

Regular formal sessions instil mindfulness muscle memory growing stronger over time. But informal practices also cultivate awareness amidst activity.


**Informal Everyday Mindfulness**

Integrating brief mindfulness into daily life activities trains the mind to snap back to presence throughout chaotic days:

-        While washing dishes, pay close attention to the warmth of the water, the sensation of suds and the dishes' smoothness. Fully immerse.

-        During routine tasks like brushing your teeth or walking to the car, bring mindful awareness to the physical sensations present. Feel the purposeful movements.

-        Waiting in lines, mindfulness can involve focusing on the feet's connection to the floor, sounds around you, feeling the breath's passage.

-        Before answering colleagues, pause to listen deeply and summon compassion. Conversations become less reactive.

-        While eating, chew slowly, savouring flavours and textures. Appreciate nourishment entering your body.


No action is too routine for mindful presence. Any activity done with full engagement enriches experience. Curiosity is the key.

Each moment unveils new discoveries about the inner and outer landscape.

## Mindfulness in Challenging Moments

Mindfulness practices prove particularly potent when challenging emotions or events arise:

-       Before reacting to upsetting situations, pause to breathe consciously. Then respond mindfully, not from fight-or-flight instinct.

-       When overcome by difficult emotions, name the feeling and accept its presence without following habitual negative thought patterns. Emotions pass like clouds.

-       Observe anger, hurt or frustration without judgement. Breathe into the sensations gently with care, allowing them to gradually dissolve. Fighting pain exacerbates it.

-       Examine painful thoughts as transient mental events, not as absolute truth. They often distort reality. Consider perspectives beyond your own.

-       Meditate when overwhelmed. Calm the body first by relaxing muscle tension through a body scan. The mind follows.

By repeatedly meeting challenges mindfully, their power to hijack attention diminishes. Peace comes from within, not outward conditions. You remain empowered, not victimised, by cultivating mindful resilience.

### Guided Meditations for Beginners

Guided meditations ease starting difficulties by verbally directing attention. Many free apps and online recordings exist. Try these classic meditations:

### Body Scan

- Systematically move attention through each area of the body from toes to head, noticing any tension or discomfort. Soften tight areas as you breathe into them. This releases up stored stress.

### Loving-Kindness

- Silently wish well-being, happiness and peace for yourself, loved ones, strangers and even enemies. This emotional warmth boosts compassion. Repeat phrases like "May you be safe; may you be happy."

### Walking Meditation

- Bring complete attention to the sensations of walking. Feel each foot lifting, moving and landing with purpose. Notice the alternating sensations. Walk slowly at a relaxed pace.

## Five Senses

-        Invest attention exploring each sense. Notice five things you see, four sounds you hear, three physical sensations, two smells and one taste sensation. This immerses you in the richness of the present.

Exploring a variety of guided meditations helps determine which resonate best. Tailor practices to suit your needs in the moment - energising, stress relief, self-compassion, etc. Results compound over time.

Deepening Practice with Breathwork

Conscious breathing exercises magnify mindfulness' benefits:

-        Diaphragmatic belly breathing stimulates the relaxation response. Exhale fully to clear stress hormones.

-        Counting breaths from 1-10 trains concentration and awareness. Begin again if the mind wanders.

-        Chanting Om on exhales vibrates the chest, calming the nervous system.

-        Alternate nostril breathing balances left/right brain hemispheres. Close one nostril, inhale through the open side, switch, repeat.

-        Breath of fire - rapidly breathe in and out through the nose, pumping the navel. Routs stagnant energy.

Ocean breath - visualise breathing in peace, breathing out stress. This cantering imagery relaxes the mind.

Regular conscious breathing reinforces the mind-body connection. Our breath reflects inner states. By directing its flow, we reshape our energy.

**In Summary**

Mindfulness provides a bridge to peace amidst the swirling demands of modern life. By setting aside formal time to ground through meditation, then infusing daily tasks with present moment awareness, we witness each experience unfolding with freshness and wisdom. Instead of endlessly chasing fulfilment, we learn to sit calmly with life exactly as it is. Breath aligns body and mind to this state of being rather than doing. With practice, mindfulness allows us to feel fully alive in each moment. Go within. What you seek is already close.

# Chapter 12: Seeking Help When Needed

Life inevitably brings periods of profound challenge and distress that strain our typical coping capacities. During such times, reaching out to access professional help, community support and human connection is essential for healing. However, stigma and avoidance often prevent people from taking the first step. This chapter explores recognizing when to seek help, the diverse resources available, and embracing assistance as an act of courage not weakness. Asking for support benefits everyone involved by fostering understanding. We all face trials alone at times, but inner peace often relies on letting others carry some weight until we grow stronger.

## Signs Professional Help May Be Needed

Certain emotional difficulties warrant seeking professional therapies and treatment plans for recovery:

- Suicidal thoughts or plans for self-harm require emergency support. Confide in trusted loved ones and call prevention hotlines.

- Symptoms of depression like lost interest in activities, appetite/sleep changes, low energy and hopelessness daily for over 2 weeks signal clinical depression. Counselling and medication help rebalance brain chemistry.

- Manic highs followed by depressive lows could indicate bipolar disorder. The shifts in mood, energy and behaviour benefit from mood stabilisers, therapy and lifestyle changes.

Panic attacks and compulsions dominating life point to anxiety disorders treatable through exposure therapy, medications and stress reduction.

-      Alcohol or drug abuse involving dependency and an inability to stop despite negative consequences. Rehab, therapy and support groups empower sobriety.

-      Trauma symptoms like flashbacks, hypervigilance and emotional numbness. Trauma-informed therapy allows safe emotional processing critical for recovery.

-      Psychosis involving breaks from reality, delusions and hallucinations may require medication and coping skill coaching.

Trust yourself. If struggling significantly, reach out. Talk to your doctor for referrals finding the right mental health professionals and treatments for your needs.


**Types of Professional Help**

Varied resources provide multifaceted support:

-      **Therapists and counsellors** - offer weekly sessions addressing mental health issues using modalities like cognitive behavioural therapy, trauma recovery, motivation strategies, etc. Match approach to your needs.

-      **Psychiatrists** - can prescribe medications like antidepressants and mood stabilisers that help rebalance brain chemistry imbalances driving conditions like anxiety, OCD and bipolar disorder. They may manage medications while you also see a therapist.

-       **Integrative medicine** - combines traditional and holistic healing like acupuncture, massage, nutrition and mindfulness. This addresses the whole person including mind, body and spirit.

-       **Support groups** - enable sharing struggles and solutions with others facing similar adversities - addiction, grief, parenting special needs children, etc. These fosters hope and best practice wisdom.

-       **Emergency psychiatric service** – provide short-term crisis intervention for suicide risk, psychosis and severe panic. Partial hospitalisation may transition individuals to less acute care.

-       **Family or couples counselling** - helps improve relational skills, communication patterns and tools for navigating conflict effectively to deepen intimacy.

Every form of support has its place in the healing process. Be open to a diverse tool kit. Integration cultivates lasting wellbeing.


## Choosing Help Aligned with Your Values

With many modalities available, select help resonating with your values, preferences and cultural background to best meet your needs:

Examine different therapeutic approaches like psychoanalytic, cognitive, humanistic, somatic, transpersonal, art and music therapy to find the right fit based on your strengths.

-        Seek providers sharing your spiritual or religious foundation if this provides comfort and a sense of interconnectedness.

-        For people of colour or LGBTQ individuals, connect with professionals well-versed in diversity issues impacting mental health to ensure deep understanding.

-        If introverted, look for therapists adept at building trust through writing, art or gentle inquiry to avoid overwhelming you.

-        For complex trauma, seek trauma-informed experts grounded in fostering safety and empowerment.

Take time to interview potential helpers via phone so you can explain your concerns and hear their approach. Aim for resonance and competency. This is a vulnerable partnership requiring trust and transparency.

### When to Seek Emergency Help

Mental health emergencies requiring immediate assistance include:

- **Expressing plans to commit suicide or end one's life**

- Acting on suicidal thoughts by taking concerning actions like giving away prized possessions.

- Experiencing psychotic symptoms like hallucinations and losing touch with reality

- Having uncontrollable panic attacks, racing thoughts or anxiety disrupting ability to function.

- Entering manic states like spending excessively, displaying poor judgement and highly impulsive behaviour. This may occur in bipolar disorder.

- Exhibiting drastic changes in personality, behaviour and mood signalling mental health decline.

In these scenarios, call emergency services, local hotlines or go to the nearest emergency room. Safety takes precedence. For non-crisis situations lacking immediate risk, calling your doctor or setting an urgent therapy appointment are safer options.


**Overcoming Barriers to Seeking Help**

Despite demonstrated benefits, many avoid accessing care. However, recognizing common obstacles makes them easier to overcome:

-        Stigma around mental illness prevents asking for support. Counter stigma through normalising struggles as part of the shared human experience. All people have challenges; some circumstances simply require more support, not judgement.

-        Doubting you are "sick enough" or your problems are insignificant. All distress that interferes with functioning deserves care. Do not wait until hitting rock bottom. Seek support early.

-        Assuming your issues are moral failings or personal weaknesses. Reframe problems as challenges needing new coping strategies, not character flaws.

-        Minimising issues and assuming you should just be able to "get over it". Trauma physically alters the brain requiring clinical interventions. Be patient with yourself.

-        Fearing treatment failure. While no instant cures exist, small consistent gains compound. Trust the process.

You deserve care. With support, even deeply entrenched wounds can mend given time and patience. Take the first step.


## The Light Amid Darkness

During times of profound despair, remember the darkness is never all-encompassing. Light always waits to be uncovered, sometimes in the most unexpected places. Possibilities exist beyond what the clouded mind presently perceives. Though you may not feel it now, you are surrounded by caring others who want to help shoulder your pain. And within you lies untapped power and purpose waiting to be discovered.

This present chapter may offer the lifeline reaching you exactly when most needed. Receive this message as a reminder you are not alone. Others have traversed this road before and emerged stronger in time. The path requires courage, compassion toward yourself, and a commitment to take each day one step at a time relying on wisdom beyond your own. By surrendering the illusion of control, receiving community support, and drawing on your deep inner reservoirs of hope, you step forward into the light.

# Appendix One - UK Resources

## Resources and further reading that might help UK residents

Potential resources for readers wishing to explore this topic further or those seeking to alleviate stress and anxiety:

### Books:

- "The Compassionate Mind" by Paul Gilbert - using CFT to manage anxiety

- "Mind Over Mood" by Christine Padesky - CBT worksheets for anxiety and depression

- "Reasons to Stay Alive" by Matt Haig - insights on managing anxiety and depression

- "The Mind Workout" by Claudia Hammond - cognitive exercises to reduce stress

### Articles:

- "How to Manage Stress" - Mind.org.uk

- "Looking After Your Mental Health" - NHS UK

- "Student Mental Health Guide" - Student Minds UK

**Online Resources:**

- Mind UK - info and support for mental health

- Rethink Mental Illness UK - services and community

- Mental Health Foundation UK - improving wellbeing

- Students Against Depression UK - for students struggling


**Support Groups:**

- Anxiety UK - support groups and online community -

  Depression UK - local support groups across the UK

- Club Drug Clinic UK - drug addiction support

- Cruse Bereavement UK - grief support helpline and groups

- Diabetes UK - diabetes community linking those living with it


**Local resources:**

- NHS Psychological Therapies Service

- Local MIND branches

- Mental health helplines

- Community centres for wellbeing classes and social groups.

## Appendix Two - Global Resources

Further resources for readers wishing to explore further this fascinating topic and for all readers seeking to alleviate stress and anxiety:

**Books**:

- "The Body Keeps the Score" by Bessel van der Kolk - a seminal book on trauma and the mind-body connection

- "The Anxiety and Phobia Workbook" by Edmund Bourne - activities and exercises for overcoming anxiety

- "The Mindfulness Solution" by Ron Siegel - techniques to manage anxiety through mindfulness

- "The Gifts of Imperfection" by Brene Brown - cultivating courage and connection amid imperfection

**Articles**:

- "Understanding the Stress Response" - Harvard Health Publishing

- "Yoga for Anxiety and Depression" - Johns Hopkins Medicine

- "Cognitive Behavioural Therapy for Anxiety" - American Psychological Association

- "The Science of Gratitude and Wellbeing" - Greater Good

Science Centre, UC Berkeley

**Online Resources:**

- Anxiety and Depression Association of America (ADAA)

- Mental Health America

- UCLA Mindful Awareness Research Centre

- Greater Good in Action - Science-based practices for wellbeing

**Support Groups:**

- Anxiety support groups - check community centres, Meetup.com, Psychology Today therapist finder

- Depression support groups - DBSA, Mental Health America, NAMI

- Addiction support groups - Alcoholics Anonymous, Narcotics Anonymous, SMART Recovery

- Grief support groups - bereavement resources at hospice centres, griefshare.org

- Chronic illness support groups - local and online communities for sharing.

# Appendix Three - Key Coping Techniques

Here are some step-by-step methods for practising key techniques from the book to alleviate stress and anxiety. Try each of these to find the one that is the most effective for you.

## Morning Mindfulness

1. Wake up 15 minutes early before jumping out of bed. Enjoy resting in the quiet.

2. Take a few deep breaths, focusing on the sensation of air filling your belly on each inhalation.

3. Feel your body lying in bed - the weight, connection with the mattress, warmth of covers.

4. Notice any sounds you hear - birds, wind, your partner's breathing.

5. Bring to mind 1-2 things you feel grateful for today.

6. Set your intention for the day - what you hope to accomplish, how you hope to interact with others.

7. Rise slowly, stretching your body before beginning morning routines.

## Progressive Muscle Relaxation

1. Get comfortable lying down or seated. Close your eyes.

2. Take a deep breath in. As you exhale, deliberately tense your feet and legs for 5-10 seconds.

3. Release the tension as you inhale again. Feel the muscles softening and notice the contrast to the tension.

4. Repeat tensing then releasing each muscle group up the body - legs, glutes, abdomen, arms, hands, shoulders, neck, jaw.

5. Finish by breathing calmly for 1 minute focused on the sensations of relaxation.

**Loving-Kindness Meditation**

1. Sit comfortably and close your eyes. Take a few centering deep breaths.

2. Silently repeat positive phrases orienting your heart and mind toward loving-kindness:

    - "May I be happy."

    - "May I be healthy."

    - "May I be safe."

    - "May I live with ease."

3. Next extend these phrases imagining loved ones:

    - "May you be happy."

    - "May you be healthy."

4. Widen the circle of compassion further to include neutral people, then difficult people. Find caring for all.

5. Repeat the phrases silently with intention, allowing the heart to open gradually. Send loving-kindness to all beings.


**Gratitude Journaling**

1. Set aside 5 minutes before bed in a quiet space.

2. Open your journal and date the entry.

3. Write down 3-5 things you felt grateful for about today. Reflect on blessings, big and small.

4. Journal any positive experiences or accomplishments from the day.

5. Describe positive emotions you had or observed in others like hope, courage, joy, excitement.

6. Consider how you could cultivate more gratitude and positive experiences tomorrow.

# References

**Progressive Muscle Relaxation**

-       Conrad, A. and Roth, W.T., 2007. Muscle relaxation therapy for anxiety disorders: It works but how? Journal of anxiety disorders, 21(3), pp.243-264.

-       Pawlow, L.A. and Jones, G.E., 2002. The impact of abbreviated progressive muscle relaxation on salivary cortisol. Biological psychology, 60(1), pp.1-16.

**Morning Mindfulness**

-       Creswell, J.D., Lindsay, E.K., Villalba, D.K. and Chin, B., 2019. Mindfulness training and physical health: Mechanisms and outcomes. Psychosomatic medicine, 81(3), p.224.

-       Lindsay, E.K. and Creswell, J.D., 2019. Mindfulness, acceptance, and emotion regulation: perspectives from monitor and acceptance theory (MAT). Current opinion in psychology, 28, pp.120-125.

**Loving-Kindness Meditation**

-       Galante, J., Galante, I., Bekkers, M.J. and Gallacher, J., 2014. Effect of kindness-based meditation on health and well-being: a systematic review and meta-analysis. Journal of consulting and clinical psychology, 82(6), p.1101.

- Leiberg, S., Klimecki, O. and Singer, T., 2011. Short-term compassion training increases prosocial behaviour in a newly developed prosocial game. Plos one, 6(3), p.e17798.

## Gratitude Journaling

- Davis, D.E., Choe, E., Meyers, J., Wade, N., Varjas, K., Gifford, A., Quinn, A., Hook, J.N., Van Tongeren, D.R., Griffin, B.J. and Worthington Jr, E.L., 2016. Thankful for the little things: A meta-analysis of gratitude interventions. Journal of Counselling Psychology, 63(1), p.20.

- Emmons, R.A. and McCullough, M.E., 2003. Counting blessings versus burdens: an experimental investigation of gratitude and subjective well-being in daily life. Journal of personality and social psychology, 84(2), p.377.